W9-AAZ-274

# Science and Your Health

## by Rebecca Weber

Content Adviser: September Kirby, CNS, MS, RN,
Instructor, Health Promotion and Wellness,
South Dakota State University

Reading Adviser: Rosemary G. Palmer, Ph.D.,
Department of Literacy, College of Education,
Boise State University

Spyglass
BOOKS

COMPASS POINT BOOKS

Minneapolis, Minnesota

Compass Point Books
3109 West 50th Street, #115
Minneapolis, MN 55410


Visit Compass Point Books on the Internet at *www.compasspointbooks.com*
or e-mail your request to *custserv@compasspointbooks.com*


Photographs ©: Corbis, cover, 10, 13; Creatas, 4; Jose Luis Pelaez, Inc./Corbis, 5; Tom Boyle/Getty
Images, 6; Unicorn Stock Photos/Tom McCarthy, 7; Tom & Dee Ann McCarthy/Corbis, 8; Image
Source, 9; Bettmann/Corbis, 11; DigitalVision, 12; Bachmann/The Image Finders, 14; Eric R.
Berndt/The Image Finders, 15; Photo Network/Esbin–Anderson, 16; Steve Kagan/Liaison/Getty Images,
17; Mark Harmel/Time Life Pictures/Getty Images, 18; Eurelios/Phototake, 19; Comstock, 20;
Independence Technology/Getty Images, 21.


Creative Director: Terri Foley
Managing Editor: Catherine Neitge
Editor: Jennifer VanVoorst
Photo Researcher: Svetlana Zhurkina
Designer: Les Tranby
Educational Consultant: Diane Smolinski



**Library of Congress Cataloging-in-Publication Data**
Weber, Rebecca.
    Science and your health / by Rebecca Weber.
       v. cm. — (Spyglass books)
Includes bibliographical references and index.
Contents: Your health—Helpful medicine—Looking inside—
Surgery—Exciting Inventions
    ISBN 0-7565-0653-0 (hardcover)
    1. Medicine—Juvenile literature. [1. Medicine.] I. Title. II. Series.
    R130.5.W43 2005
    610—dc22                                    2003024101

# Contents

NOTE: Glossary words are in *bold* the first time they appear.

# Your Health

What does science have to do with your health?

Doctors and nurses use science to help you stay healthy.

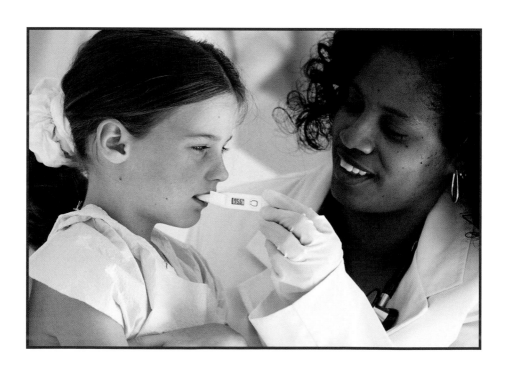

Who knows the most about your health? You do! This is why doctors ask you so many questions.

# Helpful Medicine

Long ago, doctors used plants to try to help people feel better. Sometimes the plants helped. Sometimes they did not.

Today, doctors use many different *medicines* to help people.

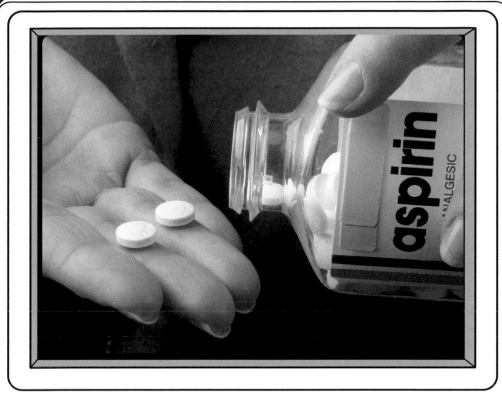

*Aspirin* is a medicine that is made from a plant. It comes from the bark of a tree.

Some medicines help people who are already sick. Other medicines keep people from getting sick.

When you were little, you probably got shots. These shots taught your body how to fight off some terrible sicknesses.

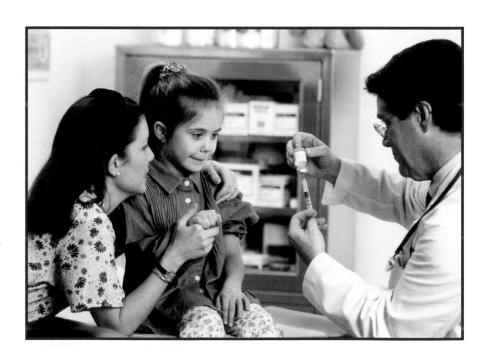

Medicines are helpful only if they are used correctly. Never take any medicine unless it is given to you by a doctor or an adult who is caring for you.

# Looking Inside

Sometimes doctors need to look inside the body to understand why a person is sick.

Doctors have machines that help them see inside the body.

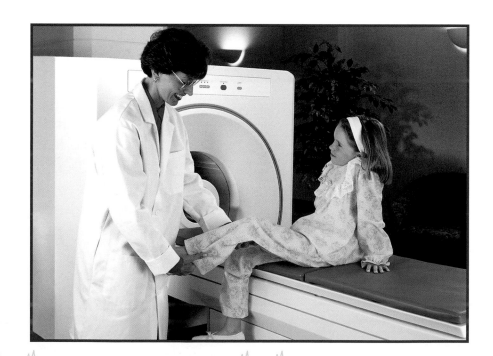

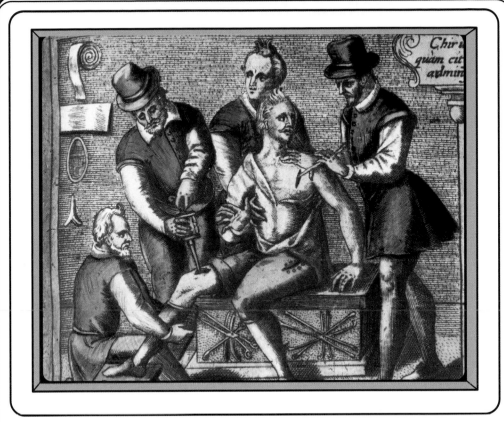

Long ago, doctors had to cut a person open in order to see inside.

Sometimes doctors use *X-rays* to see inside the body. They use these rays to take a picture of the inside of a person's body.

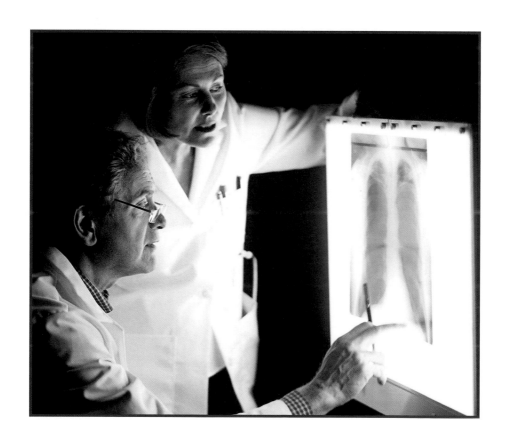

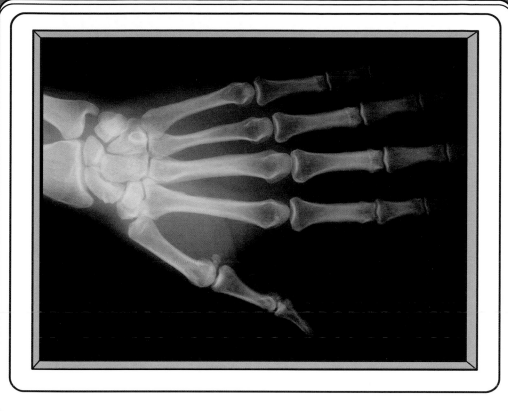

X-rays were discovered 100 years ago. At first, scientists did not know what they were. This is why they named them "X-rays."

Doctors also use *ultrasound* to see inside a person's body.

Doctors send sound waves through the body. When the waves hit something, they bounce back. A computer turns this information into a moving picture.

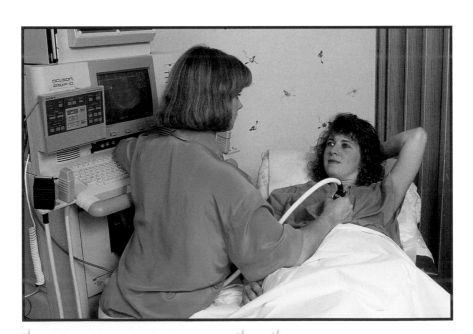

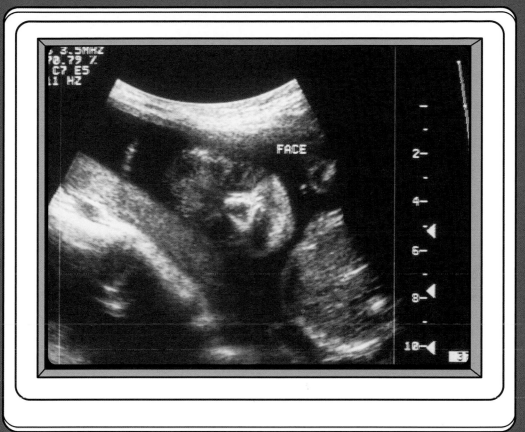

X-rays can hurt an unborn baby, but ultrasound waves are safe. This is how many mothers first see their babies!

# Surgery

Sometimes doctors need to do *surgery* to help a *patient* get better. Sometimes doctors cut into the body using a knife. Other times, they use lasers.

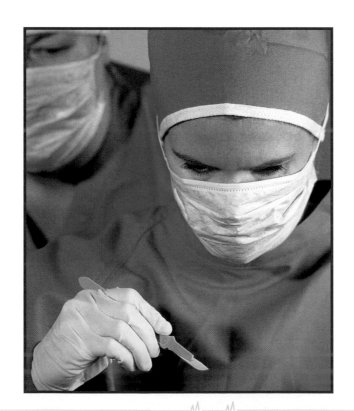

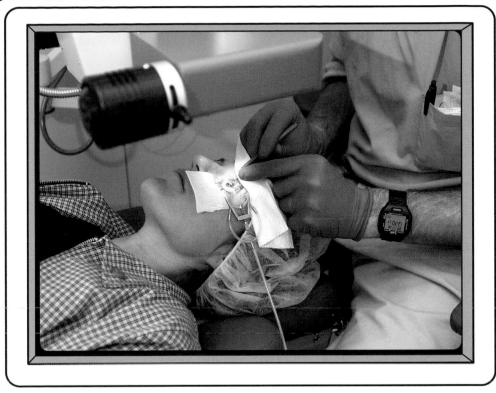

Lasers are powerful beams of light. Lasers are used for many kinds of surgeries. They can fix weak eyes or erase scars.

Today, doctors called surgeons can do many wonderful things. If someone has a heart that does not work well, a surgeon can put in a new heart that came from another person.

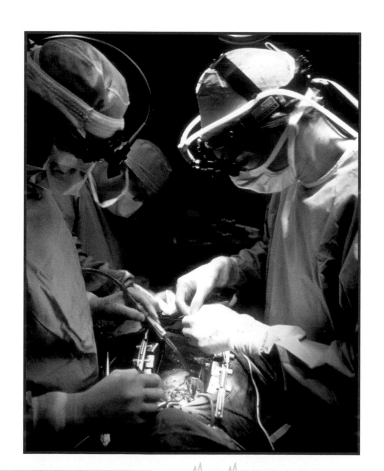

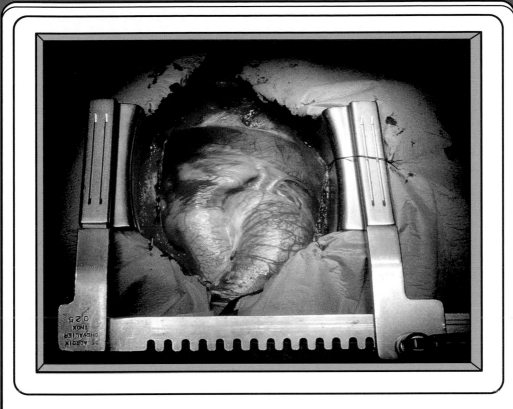

In 1967, a surgeon in South Africa was the first to successfully put another person's heart in a patient's body.

# Exciting Inventions

- *Microscopes* were invented almost 400 years ago. Doctors use them to look at *cells* from inside a person's body.

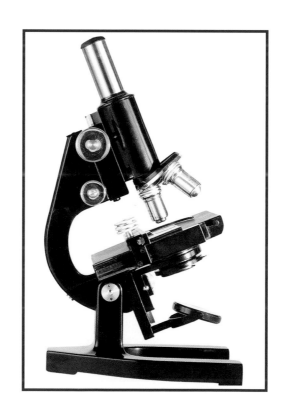

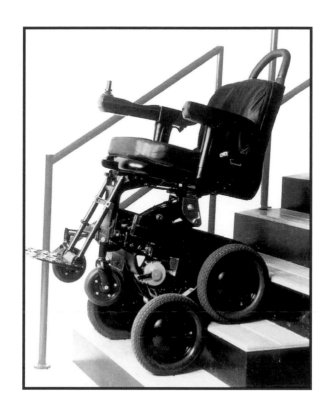

- Some wheelchairs can climb up and down stairs. They can also balance on two wheels. This makes the user as tall as a standing person.

# Glossary

*aspirin*–a medicine that helps stop pain

*cells*–the basic units of life

*medicines*–things that are used to treat
    sickness or keep people well

*microscopes*–tools used to make very small
    things big enough to see and study

*patient*–someone cared for by a doctor
    or nurse

*surgery*–when a doctor uses tools to work
    inside a person's body

*ultrasound*–sound waves beyond what people
    can hear

*X-rays*–very short waves of energy

# Learn More

## Books

Moses, Amy. *Doctors Help People.* Plymouth, Minn.: Child's World, 1997.

Schaefer, Lola M. *We Need Nurses.* Mankato, Minn.: Pebble Books, 2000.

## On the Web

For more information on *Science and Your Health,* use FactHound to track down Web sites related to this book.

1. Go to *www.facthound.com*
2. Type in a search word related to this book or this book ID: 0756506530.
3. Click on the *Fetch It* button.

Your trusty FactHound will fetch the best Web sites for you!

# Index

**GR: J**
**Word Count: 224**

# From Rebecca Weber

Whenever I travel to a new
place, I enjoy learning about
people and their daily lives. I
hope this book opens up a
little bit of the world for you!